Original title:

Pale Tunes Among the Dragon Hemp

Author: Sara Säde

ISBN HARDBACK: 978-1-80563-518-5

ISBN PAPERBACK: 978-1-80565-039-3

Songs That Linger in the Ether

Whispers danced on evening's breath,
Carried forth on twilight's crest.
Echoes of a world unseen,
Humming softly where dreams have been.

Moonlit shadows weave their song,
Notes adrift where hearts belong.
Mystic harmonies take flight,
Through the velvet cloak of night.

Stars compose their serenade,
In the quiet, truths displayed.
Winds of legend gently sigh,
As the heavens breathe and fly.

Softly sung in soft embrace,
Memories of a sacred place.
Life's enchantments softly glow,
In the ether, love's gentle flow.

Dreamers lost in timeless hues,
Chasing echoes they can choose.
Songs that linger, hearts will keep,
In the silence, dreams run deep.

Tales Woven in the Labyrinth of Night

Underneath the starlit dome,
Whispers call the wanderer home.
Paths that twist and turn in flight,
Hold the secrets of the night.

Glimmers dance in shadows cast,
Stories woven from the past.
Each turn reveals a tale untold,
In the tapestry, hopes unfold.

Moonbeams thread through darkened lanes,
Echoing the laughter, the pains.
Fables linger, spirits share,
In the hush, a breath of air.

Ancient echoes softly plead,
In the silence, hearts take heed.
Every choice a route to weave,
In the night, the soul believes.

Dreamers roam 'neath veils of dusk,
Searching for the lost, the husk.
Tales that linger in the dark,
Guide the paths that spark the heart.

Eclipses of Lost Serenades

Under the shroud of night's embrace,
Songs once sung now drift in space.
Whispers carried by the eerie wind,
In shadows deep, our dreams rescind.

Memories twine like vines on stone,
A melody lost, forever alone.
Moonbeams clutch the secrets tight,
Casting silhouettes in silver light.

Echoes flutter in the twilight air,
Chasing the tunes that linger there.
The stars, they hum a forgotten tale,
Of laughter bright and softly pale.

In each eclipse, a heartbeat sighs,
Where forgotten hopes dare to rise.
Yet silence weaves its haunting thread,
In the tapestry where dreams once led.

Embers of music fade from sight,
Captured in the lingering night.
For every note, a tear was shed,
As serenades of yore are dead.

Reverberations of the Dusk

As day recedes, the colors blend,
The sun dips low, its light to spend.
Whispers echo where shadows play,
A dance of twilight leads the way.

Murmurs rise from the fading glow,
A ballad soft, a tender flow.
Not a word must be left unsaid,
In the hush of dusk, dreams are fed.

Each breeze carries a sacred tune,
Beneath the watchful, waning moon.
Promises etched in the night sky's quilt,
Reverberations of love, love spilt.

In the stillness, the heart confides,
Secrets laid bare, as the daylight hides.
Within the dusk, old tales unfold,
Of journeys sought and hearts retold.

Yet in this moment, time stands still,
An echo held in the night's goodwill.
For as the dusk wraps the world tight,
New dreams awaken in the soft night.

Notes from a Fading World

In the quiet dusk of fading grace,
Notes weave gently, finding their place.
A symphony lost to the passage of days,
In the soft light's stop, the heart sways.

A crumbling page from a book of yore,
Where laughter sang and sorrow tore.
Each note, a trace of the life once lived,
In soft refrains, the heart feels adrift.

Mists gather round, a shroud of dreams,
A palette painted with muted themes.
The world, it whispers in shades of grey,
As hope meanders, drifting away.

Time's gentle hand erases the song,
Leaving only echoes where we belong.
Yet in each silence, a promise grows,
As fading notes set forth their prose.

Hold tight to echoes, let them not flee,
For in each note, a memory.
In the quiet, we find our way,
As notes from a fading world softly sway.

Silhouettes in the Crescent Light

Beneath the crescent's tender gaze,
Silhouettes dance in the moon's soft haze.
Figures etched in the silver glow,
A tapestry woven of dreams we know.

In the cool air, whispers unwind,
Shadows entwine, serene and kind.
Each outline tells a story fair,
In the crescent's light, free from care.

A ballet played on the night's soft stage,
Where hearts turn with every page.
The world, a stillness, seeks to comply,
As the stars anchor dreams in the sky.

Moments linger where secrets bloom,
In the cloak of night, dispelling gloom.
The crescent's light, a guiding friend,
A silhouette where stories blend.

With every breath, a promise shines,
In the silence, a melody twines.
Beneath the night, we find our might,
In the silhouettes of the crescent light.

A Serenade at the Fringes of Light

In twilight's glow, whispers parade,
Beneath the stars, secrets invade.
A serenade spun on the breeze,
Echoes of dreams, gentle and free.

Soft shadows dance, they beckon and sway,
Guiding the hearts that wander astray.
With twinkling eyes and tender sighs,
Where hopes take flight and never die.

The moonlight weaves a silver thread,
A tapestry of words unsaid.
With each sweet note, the night unfurls,
Cradling the world in whispered swirls.

In the stillness, a promise gleams,
Of magic hidden in silent dreams.
Where fate holds sway, and fortune's kiss,
Ignites the path that leads to bliss.

So let your heart be light and bright,
As you embrace the fading light.
For in the dark, there lies a spark,
A serenade that lights the dark.

Flickering Songs of the Wind's Embrace

The wind whispers soft through the trees,
A melody borne on a gentle breeze.
It sings of stories, old and wise,
Of laughter shared beneath the skies.

Flickering leaves dance in delight,
As shadows play in the fading light.
Each rustling note, a sweet refrain,
Echoes of joy, of pleasure, of pain.

A delicate waltz, the world spins round,
As dreams take flight without a sound.
In the heart's embrace, the moments weave,
A tapestry of times we believe.

Nature's orchestra, wild and free,
Plays symphonies for you and me.
With every gust, a secret shared,
A flickering song, for the hearts that dared.

So pause and listen, let the wind guide,
To where the whispers of hope abide.
For in each breath, there lies a chance,
To join the wind in a timeless dance.

The Harmony of Scattered Wishes

Beneath the canopy of twinkling stars,
A million wishes hide in jars.
Each glimmer a tale, a dream unrevealed,
In the tapestry of night, softly concealed.

A harmony flows through the silent air,
Unseen forces, a tender care.
With every heartbeat, our spirits connect,
Filling the voids that time can't neglect.

Scattered hopes like confetti twirl,
In the vast expanse of a wishing world.
Where hearts converge amidst the glow,
And secrets of love begin to flow.

Swaying gently, like petals in spring,
They whisper the joy that the night can bring.
In the quiet hush, as shadows blend,
The harmony lingers, a timeless friend.

So gather your wishes, let them take flight,
Carried on winds through the velvet night.
For in the vastness, hope will remain,
In every heartbeat, in love's sweet refrain.

Lanterns of Distant Yearning

In the twilight, lanterns glow bright,
Flickering softly in the cool night.
Guiding the lost on paths unseen,
Their glow whispers tales of what has been.

Each lantern a wish, a dream once cast,
Illuminating memories from the past.
With hearts aglow, they drift and sway,
Carrying stories of love's ballet.

Distant yearnings spark in the dark,
Each flicker ignites a waiting spark.
For in the shadows, hope finds a way,
To mend the broken, to light the gray.

So lift your gaze to the shimmering skies,
Let the lanterns guide where the spirit flies.
Embrace the night with open arms,
For in its cradle, find all your charms.

With every flicker, a promise to keep,
As dreams awaken from their sleep.
In the dance of shadows, we understand,
Lanterns of yearning, forever shall stand.

Melancholy Echoes in the Mist

In a realm where shadows cling,
Whispers weave through the night,
Lost echoes of what once was,
Fading softly from our sight.

The moon casts a silver hue,
On silken streams of dew-kissed leaves,
Memories drift like soft smoke,
Each moment a tale that weaves.

Fog wraps the world in its shroud,
Embracing dreams that never woke,
A quiet sigh beneath the trees,
Where time and silence gently spoke.

Yet in this mist, a spark ignites,
Hope brews where shadows tread,
For each heartache whispers strength,
In every tear, a seed is fed.

Lament of the Night Sky

Stars twinkle with a mournful glow,
A tapestry of tales untold,
Each flicker a wish that never soared,
Beneath the heavens, dreams unfold.

The night's breath carries silent woes,
Soft lullabies of bygone fights,
In the deep, where secrets sleep,
The universe weeps in its heights.

Clouds drift like thoughts across the way,
O'er silent realms of unseen tears,
Each shimmer a nod to the brave,
In the art of facing fears.

Yet, in the sorrow of the dark,
A comet streaks with blazing might,
Reminding souls that even night,
Can bear the weight of brilliant light.

Wistful Notes of Twilight's Embrace

As day surrenders to the dusk,
The sky blushes in gentle sighs,
Colors bleed in a soft swirl,
Where dreams dance beneath the skies.

Flickering lights adorn the path,
With whispers of the sun's farewell,
Every heartbeat's a tender note,
In twilight's magic, where spirits dwell.

The chill nips at the fading glow,
As shadows stretch their weary limbs,
Yet in this hour, hope lingers near,
Wrapped in the song of nature's hymns.

Each moment cradles a wish held tight,
In the arms of the evening's grace,
For every end gives birth to dawn,
And every twilight finds its place.

Glimmers Flickering Amongst the Ferns

Beneath the canopy of green,
Where shadows play with gentle light,
Glimmers hide in the swaying ferns,
Whispers of magic take flight.

Soft rustles tell a secret tale,
Of woodlands deep and winds so free,
Each spark a promise of joy to come,
A heartbeat shared amongst the trees.

In every nook, a wonder sleeps,
While time drips slowly like the dew,
Nature's art, a timeless dance,
Where dreams are born and whispers brew.

So wander forth beneath the boughs,
And find the glimmers in the dark,
For in the ferns, the heart can heal,
And every light ignites a spark.

Faded Memories Beneath Soft Canopies

In the hush of twilight's glow,
Whispers float where shadows grow.
Ancient trees with tales to tell,
Keep the secrets, guard them well.

Children's laughter, soft and sweet,
Echoes linger, bittersweet.
Footprints worn in earthy trails,
Each adventure holds and pales.

Beneath the blooms, the stories lie,
Of fleeting moments, by and by.
Time unfurls like petals, wide,
Memories bloom, then gently slide.

Rustling leaves and gentle sighs,
Tales of dreams where magic lies.
Underneath the arching boughs,
Faded memories, no more vows.

Night descends, a velvet shroud,
Stars awake, silver and proud.
In their light, the past ignites,
Faded dreams in moonlit nights.

Cricket Serenades and Whispered Secrets

Crickets chirp in rhythmic time,
Nature hums a gentle rhyme.
Under stars, the stories weave,
Whispers shared, hearts on sleeves.

In the grass, their symphony plays,
Echoing through twilight's haze.
Softly spoken, secrets spun,
Memories of days once begun.

Among the shadows, dreams take flight,
Glancing softly at the night.
Each note weaves the past and now,
Binding ties that time won't allow.

Fingers tracing patterns on air,
Footsteps echoing a prayer.
In the stillness, magic swells,
Cricket songs, as daylight knells.

As the moon sails high above,
Kinship thrums, a woven love.
In this dance, all fears displace,
Cricket serenades time and space.

The Language of Twilight's Breath

Twilight whispers on the wind,
A language soft, our lives rescind.
Colors blend in dusky hues,
A tranquil moment, drifting views.

Chasing shadows, dreams anew,
Night unveils what hearts pursue.
In the stillness, all is clear,
The language speaks, we bend to hear.

Glimmers of thoughts, like fireflies,
Dance alight as daylight dies.
In twilight's grasp, we find our way,
Guided gently by fading day.

Voices linger, secrets share,
Drawn together, hearts laid bare.
In the dusk, our spirits soar,
The language of the night restores.

Each breath a bond, each sigh a thread,
Twilight's charm, where dreams are fed.
In this space, our shadows blend,
In twilight's hold, we find a friend.

Lullabies Playing in the Depth of Wood

In the forest, soft and deep,
Nature sings its lullaby, sweet.
Cradled by the ancient trees,
Peace enfolds, like whispers, ease.

Moonlight dances on the stream,
Stars align, crafting a dream.
Every rustle, every sigh,
Lullabies that never die.

Through the branches, dreams take flight,
Guided softly by the night.
Sleepy creatures, nestled tight,
In their hearts, the woods ignite.

Gentle breezes murmur low,
As the silver streams still flow.
Night unfolds its sweet embrace,
Lullabies in nature's grace.

In the heart of forests wide,
Where the floral secrets hide,
Lullabies blend, sweetly spun,
In the realm where night has won.

Whispers of the Moonlit Grove

In the grove where shadows play,
Moonbeams dance and softly sway,
Whispers weave through branches high,
Breathing secrets to the sky.

Fireflies blink in hazy light,
Drawing dreams into the night,
Every sigh, a tale untold,
Woven in the silver gold.

Beneath the trees, the earth lies still,
Crickets chirp with tranquil will,
A symphony of nature sings,
While the night with magic clings.

Mossy paths and emerald leaves,
In the silence, wonder weaves,
Gentle breezes kiss the ground,
In this grove, enchantment's found.

As the night begins to fade,
Morning light, a soft cascade,
Yet the whispers linger on,
In the grove, where dreams are drawn.

Ethereal Melodies in the Night

Stars above like diamonds gleam,
In the dark, we dare to dream,
Melodies in whispers rise,
Floating soft like lullabies.

Winds carry tunes of old and wise,
Rustling leaves that gently sigh,
Notes cascade like flowing streams,
Dancing through our midnight dreams.

Every shadow hums a song,
Cloaked in night, where hearts belong,
Ethereal echoes softly play,
Guiding wanderers on their way.

In the hush, the world feels near,
Voices of the night we hear,
A harmony of life takes flight,
In the magic of the night.

As dawn approaches, melodies fade,
Yet in hearts, their songs are laid,
For every night has stories spun,
Of ethereal dreams begun.

Shadows of the Verdant Whisper

In the forest deep and vast,
Where the fleeting moments pass,
Shadows weave a mystic tale,
In the woods where dreams prevail.

Mossy paths of emerald hue,
Every step, a breath anew,
Whispers linger, soft and low,
In this place where secrets flow.

Rustling leaves in twilight's grace,
Dance like shadows in this space,
Voices murmuring through the trees,
On the soft, enchanted breeze.

Nature speaks in silent tones,
In the heart, the magic roams,
Each moment holds a quiet spark,
Lighting paths in the dark.

When the moonlight starts to fall,
Echoes answer nature's call,
In the shadows, magic calls,
Where the verdant whisper thralls.

Songs of the Enchanted Veil

Behind the veil, where dreams take flight,
Lies a world of pure delight,
Songs are sung with hearts aligned,
In this realm, the stars are twined.

Cascading laughter, soft and clear,
Trickles through the atmosphere,
Every note, a spark divine,
Threads of fate, a whispered line.

In the twilight where shadows blend,
Magic blossoms without end,
Dancing lights in harmony,
Bringing tales of mystery.

Winds carry echoes to the sky,
Enchanting secrets swirling by,
Each song a key to realms unknown,
Where the seeds of dreams are sown.

As dawn unfolds its golden hue,
Songs of the veil will guide you through,
In your heart, the echoes stay,
Of the magic found today.

Fragments of a Whispered Memory

In the hush of dusk, secrets weave,
A tapestry of echoes we believe.
Shadows dance on the cobbled street,
Where whispers cling to soft heartbeat.

Chasing dreams like moths to flame,
Each flicker a flicker of forgotten name.
Time's gentle hand, it sways so slow,
Painting memories in soft, warm glow.

Beneath the willow's sighing guise,
Lies a world hidden from weary eyes.
Fragments drift like leaves in fall,
Carrying tales that silence recalls.

In corners where moonlight cradles stars,
Magic stirs in the land of scars.
A fleeting glimpse, a shaded smile,
A moment embraced that spans a mile.

So linger here, in twilight's grace,
For memories linger in time's embrace.
In every thread, a story bends,
In whispered secrets, the heart descends.

Sighs Beyond the Gnarled Roots

Where ancient trees with twisted limbs,
Stand guard o'er secrets, dark and dim.
The roots entwine like lovers' hands,
In the heart of a world that hardly understands.

Each sigh carries a tale untold,
Of creatures lost and hearts turned cold.
The forest whispers, soft and grave,
Of wanderers seeking a path to save.

Dappled light through leaves awry,
Casts fleeting shadows as dreams pass by.
In this haven, with laughter laced,
Time slows down, and fears are faced.

Yet every thicket hides a fear,
A sigh, a sound, that lingers near.
With every step, the heart complies,
To the echo of nature's quiet sighs.

So tread with care through the tangled wane,
For beauty lies in both joy and pain.
Among the roots, let worries recede,
In the sighs of the forest, find what you need.

Soliloquy of Wandering Souls

Within the night, where shadows roam,
Wandering souls seek a forgotten home.
Each star a spark in the velvet sea,
Guiding hearts to where they're meant to be.

Beneath the cloak of the midnight sky,
Whispers linger as time slips by.
In dreams we chase what we cannot hold,
Stories written in the stars of old.

The moonlit path, a flickering guide,
Calls to the weary, the lost, the wide.
Each step a dance with the ethereal, sweet,
A ballet performed on the edge of defeat.

Yet still they roam, these souls untamed,\nThrough
valleys of sorrow, hope is named.
In shadows cast by uncertainty's hand,
They weave their truth across the land.

So pause awhile, as the night unfolds,
Hear the silence, and let it hold.
For in the soliloquy, we find our place,
In wandering hearts, we embrace grace.

Muffled Beats in the Twilight Woods

As daylight bends to evening's embrace,
The woods awaken, a secret place.
Muffled beats of life resound,
In whispers soft, where dreams are found.

Leaves rustle like soft-spoken words,
A symphony sung by unseen birds.
The twilight bathes the forest floor,
In shades of magic, we can't ignore.

Footfalls gentle on earth so deep,
Draw nearer to the shadows that sleep.
In the hush, a heartbeat draws near,
Echoes of laughter that once rang clear.

Stars begin their nightly dance,
Casting glimmers in a timeless trance.
In every corner of this sacred glade,
Muffled beats and memories trade.

So wander forth, with heart in hand,
Through twilight woods, let your spirit stand.
For in the murmurs of dusk's soft beat,
Lies a truth that makes the whole world sweet.

Whispers in the Glooming Mist

In the twilight's gentle embrace,
Soft secrets dance and weave.
A silver moon begins to trace,
The dreams that night will leave.

Through the mist where shadows sigh,
Whispers ride on the cool air.
Stars wink down from the night sky,
Enchantments linger, everywhere.

The nightingale's haunting song,
Calls the heart to a deep slumber.
In shadows dark, we all belong,
Where hopes and fears could encumber.

A flicker here, a shimmer there,
Lost in the veil of the night.
Ghostly forms swirl without care,
In the gloom, they find their light.

With each breath, the chill creeps in,
Drawing close with a knowing grin.
In the stillness, the night begins,
To share the tales of what has been.

Melodies of Wistful Shadows

Beneath the boughs where whispers play,
Shadows dance with fleeting grace.
A symphony in shades of gray,
Draws the heart to this secret place.

Glimmers of light through branches peek,
Caressing faces long forgotten.
Soft, the air begins to speak,
Of dreams held fast and loves begotten.

Echoes of laughter fill the air,
With each rustle, a memory stirs.
In the nighttime, we shed our care,
Wrapped in tales of cosmic blurs.

Misty figures glide on by,
Tales spun from the moon's soft silk.
In the twilight, not a sigh,
Breaks the magic like warm milk.

As night unwinds its gentle thread,
We follow where the music flows.
Guided by stars, not fears nor dread,
In the shadows, the heart glows.

Echoes Beneath the Twisting Vines

In the tangles where the wild things grow,
Whispers bend and sway in tune.
Beneath the boughs, secrets flow,
Like the silver light of the moon.

Twisting vines embrace the night,
Holding dreams within their clutch.
Echoes waltz in the soft twilight,
Touching hearts with a gentle touch.

The owls call through the hollow trees,
Their wisdom woven with the breeze.
Nature hums, a melodic tease,
Singing songs that bring us ease.

Flickering lights on the forest floor,
Guide the wanderer's weary feet.
Through the echoing whispers, explore,
The soft heartbeat of the night sweet.

In the still, there's magic to find,
A mingling of wonder and grace.
Beneath the vines, leave fear behind,
And find your place in this embrace.

Chords of a Forgotten Realm

In the twilight of a fading day,
Strummed strings of old begin to play.
Echoes rise from a realm unseen,
Where dreams have danced and souls have been.

With every chord, a story blooms,
Of ancient times in shadowed rooms.
Lost souls weave through the evening light,
A chorus born from the heart of night.

The gentle strum of the keeper's hand,
Calls forth spirits from golden sand.
In this realm, the lost take flight,
To revel in the endless night.

NOTES linger soft like a wistful sigh,
Encapsulating the days gone by.
A tapestry of memories spun,
In harmony with the setting sun.

So listen close, hear the song's refrain,
As the echoes dance through joy and pain.
Each chord a key to the heart's deep shell,
In a realm where forgotten tales dwell.

Serene Chanting in the Mist

In the dawn's embrace, whispers weave,
Soft echoes of dreams that we believe.
Through the mists, a melody grows,
Floating gently where the river flows.

Beneath a sky of silken gray,
The world pauses, lost in the sway.
Chants of ages long and deep,
Cradle the secrets that we keep.

With every note, the heart takes flight,
Guided by the tranquil light.
Nature's hymn calls forth the day,
In the mist where shadows play.

Each whisper sings of tales untold,
Of ancient realms and hearts of gold.
The air is thick with magic's brew,
In the quietude, hopes renew.

So listen close to the silence pure,
In that peace, we find our cure.
The mist will guide, the echoes lend,
A serenade that will not end.

Lullabies from the Forgotten Realm

In twilight's hush, the stars arise,
A lullaby of bright surprise.
From shadows of the forest deep,
Dreams take flight, and spirits leap.

Woven softly through the night,
Voices call with sweet delight.
Every note a whispered spell,
In the stillness, secrets dwell.

The moonlight bathes the glade in silver,
Where ancient beings dance and quiver.
Threads of time in rhythm sway,
As forgotten tales find their way.

Beneath the arch of starlit skies,
Imagination softly flies.
Each lullaby, a seed of hope,
Where every heart learns how to cope.

So close your eyes and hear the sound,
In dreams, the magic can be found.
From realms afar, let spirits call,
Deep in slumber, we're one and all.

Harmonies Beneath the Eldertrees

In the forest's heart, where shadows play,
The eldertrees watch the world's ballet.
With branches stretched, they whisper low,
Harmonies only the wise ones know.

Each rustle tells of memories past,
Of fleeting time that cannot last.
In sacred circles, life unfolds,
The stories of the brave and bold.

Beneath their boughs, the earth so still,
Nestled deep in nature's will.
The roots entwined in ancient lore,
A symphony we can't ignore.

The leaves, like notes, in breezes dance,
Enchanting worlds in lazy prance.
The harmonies weave a gentle charm,
Cradling us with nature's arm.

So wander close, let echoes guide,
In the eldertrees, let dreams abide.
In every sigh, the past will teem,
Sing along to the forest's dream.

Luminous Threads of Time

In the tapestry of night so bright,
Luminous threads weave tales in light.
Each shimmer holds a glimpse of gold,
Stories of the brave and bold.

Through the ages, whispers flow,
Carried on the winds that blow.
Time unfurls in a cosmic dance,
Inviting all to take a chance.

Stars like eyes, they watch and gleam,
Guardians of the waking dream.
In their glow, the past aligns,
As destiny begins to shine.

Each moment captured in silver lines,
Entwined with fates that fate defines.
In every heartbeat, echoes chime,
Luminous threads of endless time.

So hold your dreams and let them soar,
In the fabric of the evermore.
For every wish, a star will guide,
In the dance where worlds abide.

An Elegy of Unseen Currents

In shadows draped, the whispers glide,
Of tales untold, where secrets bide.
A river flows beyond the sight,
With echoes soft, and heart's delight.

The moon, a keeper of the dreams,
Sways gently on the silver streams.
A sigh from depths, where waters churn,
In silence lost, our hearts, they yearn.

Beneath the stars, the spirits weave,
A tapestry of night, we grieve.
For all that's passed, we shed a tear,
In currents deep, we feel them near.

Yet in the dark, hope finds its spark,
As dawn will break, dispelling dark.
For every end gives rise anew,
In unseen flows, our love holds true.

So here we stand, no more forlorn,
With love reborn, from shadows torn.
In unseen currents, life will flow,
A gentle tide, forever glow.

Dances of the Gloaming Shade

Beneath the boughs where twilight plays,
The shadows dance in soft arrays.
A flicker here, a shimmer there,
With whispers sweet, they fill the air.

The nightingale starts its refrain,
While crickets hum a soft-worn strain.
In this embrace, the world feels bright,
As stars abound, in velvet night.

The gloaming shade invites the heart,
To find its pulse, to feel the art.
In every sway, a story told,
Of fleeting times, of dreams of old.

So let us twirl in shadows deep,
Where ancient woods their secrets keep.
In dances shared, we'll lose our cares,
As laughter's light fills tender airs.

In every step, remember well,
The magic dwells where shadows dwell.
With each embrace, our spirits rise,
In gloaming shade, we'll find the skies.

Tones Echoing through Darkened Glades

In quiet depths where echoes call,
The forest sings, a haunting thrall.
With every rustle, every sigh,
A gentle song beneath the sky.

Through darkened glades, the tones resound,
In harmony with earth and ground.
The wind, a bard of tales untold,
Weaves through the branches, brave and bold.

A waltz of leaves in moonlight's beam,
Dances of dusk, a dreamer's dream.
With every note, the night unfolds,
A magic spun, like spun gold.

In whispers soft, the night takes flight,
Through shadows dim, we find our light.
For in the dark, our hearts will sing,
Of brighter days and love's sweet spring.

So linger now, in glades so deep,
And let the echoes soothe your sleep.
For in their tones, we find our way,
Through every night, to greet the day.

Mysterious Melodies of the Veiled Night

In hush of night, the veil descends,
With melodies that time suspends.
The stars, they twinkle, secrets share,
In whispers soft, in moonlight's glare.

The shadows play, a ghostly band,
Each note a touch of hidden hand.
With voices wrapped in silken thread,
The dreams arise, from tears we've shed.

Through glistening leaves, the sounds will flow,
A siren's call, where moonbeams glow.
In every tone, a story spun,
The night unfolds, as dreams begun.

In veiled embrace, we find our peace,
Where thoughts like ripples never cease.
A tapestry of night surrounds,
In silent wonder, life abounds.

So listen close, the night will sing,
Of whispered hopes and endless spring.
In melodies where mysteries hide,
We'll find the dreams we've sought inside.

Resounding Echoes in the Stillness

In the hush of night, whispers weave,
Stars above twinkle, begin to believe.
Every shadow stretches, time holds its breath,
Melodies linger, stolen from death.

Twilight dances, cloaked in a shroud,
Voices of ancients, both solemn and loud.
With every heartbeat, the echoes collide,
In the stillness, the past will reside.

Through tangled branches, secrets unfold,
Stories of courage, tales yet untold.
The moonlight bathes all in a serene glow,
While dreams of the lost through the silence flow.

Beneath the old oaks, shadows entwine,
Glimmers of laughter, a memory's sign.
Resounding echoes, like whispers of time,
Carried on winds, in rhythm, in rhyme.

So heed the stillness, where magic remains,
In the heart of the night, nothing but gains.
In the absence of noise, a wonder is spun,
In this quietude, we become one.

Dreams Entwined with Shadow Play

In the twilight hour, dreams softly sigh,
Beneath drifting clouds, where the lost spirits lie.
A canvas of shadows, painted with care,
Each flicker of hope, a moment to share.

Whispers of wishes beneath silver skies,
Twinkling like stars, where imagination flies.
In the dance of the dark, secrets we chase,
Illusions inviting us into their embrace.

As dreams intertwine with the night's gentle glow,
They weave through the starlight, like rivers flow.
Phantoms of laughter echo in air,
In shadow's embrace, we have not a care.

With every heartbeat, new worlds appear,
Eldritch encounters, both wondrous and clear.
Lost in this moment, our spirits shall sway,
As we waltz through the night, in shadow play.

Soon dawn will come, unveiling the light,
Yet in this enchantment, our hearts take flight.
Tomorrow may call, but still we might stay,
In the weave of our dreams where shadows hold sway.

The Sonata of Wandering Spirits

In the misty glade, they softly hum,
Wandering spirits, a ritual drum.
Each note a story, a time long gone,
Under the stars, the night carries on.

With breath of the night, their chorus ignites,
Lively and vibrant, like ethereal lights.
Each whisper a longing, a memory's plea,
Caught in the echoes, forever set free.

They dance with the shadows, a graceful ballet,
Around ancient trees, where the lost find their way.
In flickers of starlight, their laughter rings clear,
The sonata of spirits, for none but us here.

As melodies twine through the soft evening air,
Tales of their journeys, they tenderly share.
With every crescendo, we're drawn to the night,
Entranced by their musings, in tranquil delight.

So linger a moment, let your heart take flight,
In this sonata, find peace in the night.
For in wandering spirits, we meet our own soul,
In the music of silence, we become whole.

Murmurs from the Enchanted Thicket

In the depths of the woods, where secrets reside,
Murmurs of magic and mysteries bide.
Leaves softly rustling, a gentle refrain,
Whispers of wonder, like a lover's lane.

Beneath emerald canopies, shadows embrace,
Tales of enchantments drift through timeless space.
As creatures forgotten in moonlit retreats,
Spill forth their stories where the wild heart beats.

From the thickets emerge, soft echoes of lore,
The dance of the fae at the heart of the core.
Each flicker of warmth through the cool evening air,
Is a promise of magic, spun with tender care.

As dawn creeps closer, with colors aglow,
Nature's own symphony begins to bestow.
Murmurs from thickets, where dreams intertwine,
Guide the lost wanderers back to the divine.

So pause for a moment, let your spirit soar,
In the enchanted embrace, find what you adore.
For in every murmur, a chance to be free,
In the heart of the thicket, seek your true glee.

Choir of the Enigmatic Breeze

Whispers weave through the ancient trees,
A melody carried on the gentle breeze.
Swaying leaves hum a soft refrain,
Secrets flutter like shadows in the lane.

Moonlight dances on the forest floor,
Casting glimmers at forgotten lore.
Echoes of laughter, faint and sweet,
As woodland creatures gather to greet.

The twilight sings, a haunting song,
Inviting wanderers to sing along.
In every rustle, a tale unfolds,
Of magic hidden and adventures bold.

Stars peek through the shimmering veil,
Guiding footsteps on this mystic trail.
With every breath, the night awakes,
As dreams take flight, the heart forsakes.

In harmony with the night's soft kiss,
The breeze carries whispers of bliss.
Join the choir, let your spirit soar,
In the embrace of the forest's lore.

Faint Harmonies Beneath the Stars

Beneath the vast and twinkling skies,
Soft melodies weave and rise.
Songs of dusk as day departs,
Charming whispers that warm our hearts.

In the stillness, dreams begin,
With every star, a new world spins.
We join the dance of night's embrace,
Finding solace in this sacred space.

Laughter travels on the night air,
Floating gently without a care.
A symphony of silence profound,
In every shadow, magic is found.

Follow the notes that softly gleam,
In midnight's overture, lose the dream.
With every heartbeat, the cosmos sighs,
In the lullaby of the endless skies.

Faint harmonies, a woven thread,
Binding souls in the dreams we tread.
Let starlit whispers guide our way,
In the soft embrace of night and day.

The Language of the Hidden Grove

In the curve of ancient roots, we meet,
Where secrets breathe through verdant seat.
A language spoken in rustling leaves,
Whisp'ring tales that the forest weaves.

Sunlight dapples the emerald ground,
Where every heartbeat can be found.
Footsteps echo on the mossy trails,
Carving stories where silence prevails.

Crickets sing in the early dusk,
Their symphony wrapped in the twilight musk.
Every shadow bears a shimmering glow,
The hidden grove, where wonders flow.

In a world awash with dreams untold,
Voices of the forest beckon bold.
Listen close, for wisdom speaks,
In the every branch and the rustling creeks.

The language dances on the air,
Binding us in a bond so rare.
With every sigh, we lean to hear,
The grove's embrace, forever near.

Echos of the Fae Realm

Cloaked in mystery, the fae do play,
Painting shadows at the end of day.
With laughter ringing through a twilight spell,
In every corner, a story to tell.

Fluttering wings in the moonlit mist,
Whispers of magic that can't be missed.
Dancing lights lead the curious souls,
To a realm where enchantment unfolds.

Woven glades and shimmering streams,
The fae weave life into our dreams.
In their garden, where time stands still,
Every heartbeat bends to their will.

With glimmers of joy in the twilight air,
The fae entice us with charms to share.
Among the flowers and sparkling dew,
Realms intertwine, old and new.

Echos linger long after they've gone,
Tracing paths of magic drawn.
In the heart of night, we hear their song,
Where the fae belong, we all belong.

Enchanted Shadows

In twilight's hush, the shadows dance,
A whisper of magic, a fleeting chance.
Beneath the trees where secrets weave,
The heart of the forest begins to believe.

Glimmers of starlight, flickers of grace,
Each path illuminated, a warm embrace.
Ancient tales spun on the breeze,
The night sings softly, putting souls at ease.

With every step, the spirits hum,
In enchanted woods, where wonders come.
Lost in the twilight, we find our way,
Through shadows that linger till break of day.

A tapestry woven with dreams in sight,
In this realm of magic, we take flight.
For hidden within the shadows' play,
Are secrets that beckon, come what may.

So hold your breath, let the journey start,
Let echoes of wonder enkindle your heart.
As night's cloak drapes, and the stars unroll,
Feel the enchantment ignite your soul.

Silenced Echoes

Within the quiet where echoes sleep,
Lies a treasure of stories, buried deep.
Silenced voices of ages gone,
Whispering secrets, a forgotten song.

Through shadows of silence, they weave their thread,
Tales of the living, the spirit, the dead.
In every heartbeat, in every sigh,
The memories linger, refusing to die.

Beneath the surface, in soil and stone,
Lies a world where the lost are never alone.
In the rustle of leaves, the crack of the earth,
We find their stories, their laughter, their mirth.

Each breath of wind, a soft caress,
Reviving the souls that once knew success.
In the quiet darkness, we learn to listen,
To tales of love and the light that glistens.

So when the night falls and the stillness grows,
Remember the echoes, for each one knows.
In the silence, there's beauty, a bond we share,
A tapestry woven with heartfelt care.

Embrace the forgotten, let their memories flow,
For in silenced echoes, great truths still glow.

The Rhythm of Moonlit Whispers

In the hush of night, whispers arise,
Carried aloft beneath silver skies.
The rhythm of secrets in shadows they weave,
A melody tender, inviting to believe.

Moonlight cascades on the glistening dew,
Bringing to life what we once knew.
With every heartbeat, the whispers grow,
Guiding our steps where the soft breezes blow.

Dancing with dreams in the twilight's hold,
Stories unfurl as the night unfolds.
Each note, a heartbeat, each sigh, a prayer,
In the moonlit glow, we find solace there.

Through glades enchanted, we wander far,
Drawn by the light of a gentle star.
Every rustle, every sigh,
Is woven with magic, as we drift by.

The night speaks softly to those who will hear,
In the rhythm of whispers that draw us near.
So chase the shadows, let your heart sway,
For the moonlit whispers will guide the way.

Twilight's Canvas of Lost Melodies

As twilight fades, the day retreats,
Painting the sky with dusky feats.
A canvas adorned with colors so bright,
Hiding the echoes of fading light.

In the stillness, music softly plays,
A symphony woven from golden days.
Lost melodies drifting on gentle air,
Whispers of moments that spark memories rare.

Each stroke of color tells tales untold,
Of laughter and love, of the young and old.
The canvas alive, each hue echoes,
The stories of lives where the river flows.

As dreams intermingle and shadows blend,
Twilight's embrace will always extend.
The canvas of night holds secrets in trust,
And within its depths, we find what was just.

So linger a moment, let the evening weave,
A tapestry rich with what hearts believe.
In twilight's embrace, let us softly dream,
For lost melodies linger, more real than they seem.

WIth each passing moment, as night descends,
Remember the songs where the journey bends.
In twilight's canvas, life paints its mark,
Crafting forever in the softening dark.

Rhapsody of the Enchanted Glade

In a glade where whispers dance,
The moonlight weaves a silken trance.
Fireflies twinkle in the night,
As shadows play in soft twilight.

Gentle breezes carry tales,
Of ancient woods and secret trails.
A symphony of rustling leaves,
As magic stirs and softly breathes.

Mossy carpets, lush and green,
Hide mysteries yet to be seen.
Each footstep echoes, soft yet clear,
Calling forth the spirits near.

With every note the owls do sing,
A serenade of everything.
Stars above begin to gleam,
Entwined in nature's woven dream.

So linger here beneath the trees,
And let your heart dance in the breeze.
For in this place where wonders thrive,
The enchanted glade comes alive.

Strumming the Heartstrings of Twilight

As day surrenders to the night,
The stars begin their gentle flight.
With every strum and whispered sigh,
The twilight sings a lullaby.

Crickets join the fading light,
Their melodies take sudden flight.
A hush falls soft on meadow wide,
Where secrets of the day abide.

The horizon blushes, deep and red,
Painting dreams where fears have fled.
The world transforms in mystic hue,
Each moment feels both old and new.

Glimmers of gold, a fleeting grace,
Shadows waltz in this sacred space.
As the night unfurls its cloak,
The heartstrings pull, the silence spoke.

Like gentle whispers in the dark,
Every heartbeat leaves its mark.
The evening drapes its velvet charm,
And wraps the world in tender arms.

Songs of the Almost Forgotten

In the corners of the mind,
Lie the songs we left behind.
Embers glow in distant past,
Whispers of a time that danced.

Fading echoes, soft and sweet,
Carry warmth on fragile feet.
Each note a story, a fleeting ghost,
Weaving magic, holding close.

In the silence, shadows loom,
Flickering like a fading bloom.
Yet in the heart, they still reside,
With memories that never died.

Listen close to the gentle breeze,
It hums of love and heart's unease.
The past, a treasure, vast and wide,
In every heartbeat, it abides.

So take a moment, breathe it in,
The quiet songs echo within.
Each melody, a token true,
Of almost forgotten, still new.

A Tapestry of Murmured Dreams

Beneath the veil of starlit skies,
Where dreams awaken, softly rise.
Threads of silver, gold so bright,
Weave the fabric of the night.

Whispers linger in the air,
A tapestry beyond compare.
Each secret sewn, each hope unspooled,
In this realm, our hearts are schooled.

Fleeting visions dance and twine,
In a world where souls align.
With every sigh, a wish takes flight,
In the symphony of night.

Cradled dreams on starlit streams,
Flow like water, soft as beams.
A world adorned in shimmering seams,
Bound together by murmured dreams.

So close your eyes, embrace the gleam,
And wander deep into the dream.
For in this realm of silent schemes,
We weave our lives in whispered themes.

A Symphony of the Whispering Winds

In the vale where shadows play,
The winds weave tales both old and grey,
With whispers soft, they dance and twine,
A symphony of the earth's design.

Through ancient trees, their secrets flow,
In every rustle, stories grow,
A chorus sung by nature's breath,
A hymn of life, entwined with death.

Above the peaks, where eagles soar,
The winds carry dreams from distant shores,
They lift the heart, they soothe the mind,
In their embrace, all hopes combined.

Through starlit nights, their voices weave,
A tapestry of what we believe,
In every breeze, a promise lies,
A lullaby beneath the skies.

So if you listen, close your eyes,
You'll hear the winds' enchanting sighs,
In every rustle, life unfolds,
A symphony of tales retold.

Chants from a Shrouded Haven

In a cloistered glen where shadows fall,
The whispers artfully heed the call,
Chants weave like smoke, soft and slow,
In twilight's embrace, they gently flow.

Moss-clad stones hold secrets deep,
Where fallen leaves in silence sleep,
Echoes linger, a haunting song,
In this shrouded haven, we belong.

The moon peeks through a tempest's veil,
Casting light on the whispered tale,
In the hush, a spirit's breath,
Alive within the arms of death.

Through tangled roots, the chants ascend,
An ancient magic begins to blend,
With every note, the air ignites,
A canvas painted in starry nights.

So hold your breath, and let it be,
For in this haven, we are free,
In every chant, a world awakes,
A sacred bond that never breaks.

Melodic Fables of the Ancient Soil

On ancient soil where stories grow,
Roots intertwine, and wisdom flows,
Melodic fables, rich and deep,
In every furrow, secrets keep.

The harvest moon shines bright above,
As earth rejoices in tales of love,
Voices linger in the fields so wide,
Where time and memory gently bide.

With every dawn, the sun unveils,
A symphony of nature's trails,
In every whisper, life awakes,
The pulse of earth in rhythmic shakes.

From rooted trees to mountains high,
The fables echo, never shy,
A tapestry of life, adorned,
In soil and sun, forever sworn.

So heed the call of the earthy song,
In every heartbeat, we belong,
For in this land, both wild and free,
The ancient soil tells you and me.

Cadence of the Silvery Dew

At dawn's embrace, the world is new,
A gentle sway of silvery dew,
In softest light, it sparkles bright,
A cadence born of morning's light.

Each droplet sings on petals fair,
A lullaby, beyond compare,
With every glint, a promise kept,
In nature's arms, where dreams are slept.

The breeze carries a fragrant tune,
As sunlight dances, a golden rune,
In the stillness, hear the call,
The cadence of life embraces all.

Through meadows wide, in whispers sweet,
The silvery dew will guide our feet,
With every step, a journey starts,
A melody that lifts our hearts.

So bask in the beauty, let it stay,
In the cadence of dawn's ballet,
For each new day, a song awakens,
In silvery dewdrops, love unshaken.

Hues of Twilight's Lament

Beneath the veil of fading light,
Whispers dance in the creeping night.
Colors bleed in a spectral glow,
As the stars above begin to show.

A lullaby from the setting sun,
Crickets chirp, the day is done.
Shadows stretch, as silence falls,
The twilight's grace in twilight's calls.

Golden hues blend into blue,
Dreamers travel where shadows grew.
With every sigh from the dusk's embrace,
The twilight holds a hidden grace.

Eclipsed by clouds, the moon peeks through,
Casting glimmers of silver dew.
A tapestry woven from dusk till dawn,
In twilight's arms, the magic's drawn.

Through melancholy's sweet refrain,
Each whispered note, a hint of pain.
Yet in the dark, a spark ignites,
Hues of love flood the moonlit nights.

Songs from the Elder Grove

In the heart of the woods, the ancients sing,
Melodies echo, as shadows take wing.
Branches sway to the rhythm of breeze,
The elder grove whispers among the trees.

Voices of ages through roots interlace,
Stories of love, of loss, and of grace.
With each note, the spirits arise,
In fragrant blooms where time never dies.

Softly the night wraps its cloak around,
Echoing laughter from hidden ground.
Winding paths of enchantment and lore,
Lead the lost to the grove evermore.

With each song, the world fades away,
As twilight calls them to softly sway.
In every leaf, a tale to unfold,
Of dreams forgotten and wishes bold.

Crickets and owls join the refrain,
In the elder grove, where hearts then remain.
Nature's choir in harmony glows,
Songs from the woods where the wildflower grows.

Rhythms of the Whispering Leaves

In the murmuring hush of a twilight breeze,
The leaves confide their secret pleas.
Rustling softly, their voices unite,
With stories woven from day into night.

Each flickering shadow forms a new tale,
Where dreams take flight and fears grow pale.
The rhythms of nature, a timeless song,
Whispered truths where hearts belong.

Beneath the boughs that dance and sway,
The pulse of the world keeps darkness at bay.
With every gust, the leaves reply,
In sonorous waves, beneath the sky.

A chorus of whispers in twilight's embrace,
Eases the soul with its tender grace.
For in each rustle, there's magic unfurled,
Rhythms that bind both the night and the world.

Stories of ages in each gentle fall,
The heartbeat of nature, a part of us all.
Listen closely, they teach us to weave,
The tapestries born in the whispering leaves.

Harmonies of the Ethereal Night

As starlight drapes the ethereal sea,
The night unfolds in a vibrant spree.
Each twinkle ignites a familiar song,
Echoes of joy where the heart feels strong.

Moonbeams shimmer on water's embrace,
Casting soft shadows upon each face.
Harmony lingers in whispers so clear,
In every breath, the magic draws near.

The tapestry woven from dark into light,
Weaves together all creatures of night.
An orchestra plays with a ghostly hand,
Harmonies rise from the shimmering land.

Under the dome of a velvet sky,
Each note a promise that never will die.
A lull in the darkness, a world set free,
Harmonies change the way we see.

With every dawn, we bid goodbye,
To the symphony sung by the starlit sky.
Yet deep in our hearts, the echoes remain,
Of night's sweet melodies, a beautiful chain.

Songs of the Wandering Spirits

In twilight's glow, the whispers weave,
Echoes of tales that spirits leave.
Through the mists, their voices glide,
In the shadows, they confide.

Through ancient woods, they take their flight,
Chasing dreams beyond the night.
Their laughter dances, soft and sweet,
A gentle song, a rhythmic beat.

With every rustle in the trees,
A hint of magic on the breeze.
They call out names long lost to time,
In haunting tones, they softly rhyme.

Among the stars, their secrets spin,
With every heartbeat, tales begin.
The moonlight weaves a silken thread,
Where echoes linger, fear and dread.

So listen close when night descends,
For the spirits roam where daylight ends.
Their songs entwined with dreams we share,
In the silence, they linger there.

Enchanted Echoes from the Thicket

In thickets deep, where shadows play,
The echoes hold the light of day.
Flickering whispers, soft and clear,
Unravel tales that we all hear.

Beneath the leaves, a world alive,
With sparkling dreams that seem to thrive.
In every rustle, secrets hide,
Beckoning hearts to come inside.

The wind carries a haunting tune,
As fireflies twinkle 'neath the moon.
Each echo dances, wild and free,
In this enchanted tapestry.

Through tangled vines, the path unwinds,
With stories woven, fate entwined.
In twilight's hush, the magic gleams,
A world alive with whispered dreams.

So step with care, and tread with grace,
For every echo holds a trace.
Of lives once lived and love's embrace,
In thickets deep, a sacred space.

Reverberations of the Flora's Heart

In fields of green, where flowers sway,
The flora sings in bright array.
With colors bold and scents divine,
Their beauty calls, a sweet design.

Each petal holds a promise true,
Of sunlit skies and morning dew.
In every bud, a tale is spun,
Of whispered hopes beneath the sun.

The roots entwined in earth so deep,
Guard stories that the silence keep.
With gentle grace, the breezes blow,
Awakening dreams that softly grow.

The whispers rise like songbirds' flight,
In harmony, they greet the night.
Their reverberation, a symphony,
Of nature's heart, forever free.

So when you roam through fragrant glades,
Listen close to the serenades.
For in the flora's vibrant art,
Lie the echo's of nature's heart.

The Soothing Silence of Hidden Realms

In hidden realms where silence reigns,
The stillness hums in gentle strains.
A tranquil peace envelops all,
Within the soft, mysterious hall.

The air is thick with secrets old,
With stories waiting to be told.
In shadowed corners, dreams take flight,
Beneath the watchful stars at night.

With every breath, the whispers sigh,
In echoes faint, they seem to cry.
For in this stillness, worlds collide,
With magic swirling deep inside.

Each flicker of a candle's light,
Reveals the paths of lost delight.
A soothing silence, soft and sweet,
Where echoes fade, and moments meet.

So wander through these hidden lands,
And feel the magic in your hands.
For in the silence, tales unfold,
In hidden realms, a wonder bold.

The Lilt of Half-Remembered Nights

In whispers soft, the stars align,
A tapestry of dreams, entwined.
The moon, a lantern, guides our flight,
Through velvet skies of deepest night.

With every breath, the memories flow,
Like silver streams where echoes glow.
Fleeting shadows, memories twine,
In the lilt of half-remembered time.

We dance through corridors of fate,
Where laughter lingers, love is weight.
Each fleeting glance, a story told,
In dreams that shimmer, brave and bold.

The nightingale sings a haunting tune,
While fireflies twinkle, a fleet platoon.
In the embrace of starlit grace,
We wander on, lost in this place.

In whispered secrets, worlds collide,
Where hope is found, and faith abides.
Through every shadow, every ray,
The night will always hold its sway.

Threads of Echoing Silence

In corners dark, the silence threads,
A quiet hum, where shadows tread.
With each heartbeat, softly sewn,
A fabric spun from dreams alone.

Echoes flutter like feathers light,
In the stillness of the night.
With gentle hands, we weave our fears,
Into the tapestry of years.

The world outside fades to a hush,
As moonbeams take their subtle brush.
Every pause, a story waits,
In the echo of forgotten fates.

With every breath, the stillness speaks,
In whispers soft, and gentle peaks.
Stars above, a watchful guise,
As we unearth the buried lies.

In the dance of shadows, time is spun,
With every sigh, a life begun.
Through threads of silence, we shall find,
The echoes of our heart, entwined.

Chimes of the Ancients

In the distance, chimes resound,
Through the ages, wisdom found.
Ringing clear, a timeless song,
Where every heart has belonged.

The ancients whisper through the trees,
In rustling leaves, in gentle breeze.
Their stories inked in nature's skin,
Where every tale, a world within.

With each vibration, truths arise,
Echoing through the sprawling skies.
Time weaves its magic, ever bold,
In the chimes of secrets, softly told.

As twilight dims and day departs,
The chimes awaken longing hearts.
In the swirling mist of fading light,
The ancients beckon, drawing night.

We listen close, though shadows fall,
To the timeless tales of one and all.
In the symphony of night's embrace,
The chimes resound, a sacred space.

Shadows Dancing Beneath the Moon

Beneath the moon, shadows entwine,
In a ballet, both dark and fine.
With every sweep across the floor,
They spin and twirl, forevermore.

The night is alive with stories untold,
Whispers of daring, wise and bold.
As stars watch o'er this whispered trance,
The shadows sigh and quietly dance.

Each flicker of light a fleeting glance,
Guiding the night in a velvet romance.
With shadows beating like a heart,
We find ourselves, each playing our part.

The moonlight spills on whispered grace,
In this sanctuary, we find our place.
With open arms, we chase our fears,
As shadows dance throughout the years.

Together we weave, the night a loom,
Stitching our dreams in the shadow's gloom.
Beneath the moon's soft, watchful gaze,
We dance with shadows through the haze.

Dreams Ensnared in Gossamer Threads

In twilight's embrace, shadows entwine,
A whisper of starlight, a sparkle benign,
Slumbering hopes, like threads in the night,
Captured in dreams, they take graceful flight.

Through meadows of silver and pools of soft glow,
Where secrets of ages in silence bestow,
Each flickering moment, a delicate dance,
Threads woven softly, invoking a chance.

The moon casts her gaze on the slumbering earth,
A cradle of wonders, a realm of rebirth,
While echoes of laughter drift gently above,
Ensnared in the gossamer, cradled by love.

As morning awakes, with a sigh of release,
The dreams softly vanish, yet grant us some peace,
Though hidden may be all those visions we seek,
Their essence, like whispers, continues to speak.

So hold fast your dreams, let them twirl in your mind,
For threads woven tightly will never unwind,
In the tapestry woven, a story prevails,
Of dreams snug and safe, in our hearts, they set sails.

Soft Lullabies of the Wandering Spirits

Beneath a vast sky where the wild stars sing,
Wandering spirits in moonlight take wing,
With voices like rivers, they weave through the trees,
Soft lullabies float on the warm evening breeze.

They hum of the moments that once passed us by,
Whisper their secrets and bid us goodbye,
The echoes of laughter, the shadows that play,
In the stillness of night, they guide us away.

Through valleys of twilight, where shadows will blend,
They wander together, they meet without end,
With stories of old, and a sparkle of light,
They dance through the meadow, a breathtaking sight.

Each note that they carry, a promise of peace,
In soft lullabies, our troubles release,
As heartbeats align with the rhythm they share,
The spirits remind us, we're never nowhere.

So listen for whispers, in stillness abide,
The soft lullabies that the night shall provide,
As dreams drift like smoke, in the glow of the moon,
Let spirits enfold you, as night turns to noon.

Ballads of the Sylvan Realm

In the forest's embrace, where the green shadows weave,
A melody echoes, what hearts can believe,
The ballads of nature, rich tales carved in bark,
Sing fiercely of magic that brightens the dark.

The dance of the leaves sings with every soft gust,
While streams clap their hands in a ripple of trust,
Each creature a note in this symphonic throng,
They share ancient secrets in harmony's song.

With lanterns of fireflies guiding the way,
Through twilight's embrace, where giggling sprites play,
Every whisper of winds, a soft lull to the heart,
In ballads of sylvan, the dreamers take part.

Twilight unveils a tapestry bold,
With threads spun of hope and of stories once told,
The owls hoot along with the crickets sweet tune,
In the sylvan realm, each magic-bloomed moon.

So let the soft echoes find purchase within,
Embrace the old ballads, where dreams may begin,
For the heart of the forest forever shall keep,
The magic of moments forever in deep.

Wails of the Lonesome Faeries

In twilight's glow, where soft shadows play,
The lonesome faeries weave stories of gray,
With wings made of whispers, they flutter and sigh,
Wailing for lost dreams that drift softly by.

Each tear they release flows like silver in dew,
A lament for the hopes that once danced in their view,
In hidden glades where the moonlight won't go,
They weave their sad ballads of love long ago.

Their hearts fill with longing, for friendships once bright,
As they sing to the stars that adorn the night,
Through circles of petals, they twirl 'neath the trees,
A symphony haunting, yet gentle as breeze.

With echoes of laughter that once filled the air,
Linger the traces of faeries' despair,
Each sighing lament, a song of release,
In the grove where the shadows conceal and appease.

So heed the soft wails that drift on the air,
For the lonesome faeries trace stories of care,
Woven in moonlight, where dreams intertwine,
In the heart of the forest, their spirits shall shine.

When the Nightingale Weeps

In twilight glades where shadows creep,
The nightingale begins to weep.
Her song, a tune of endless night,
Echoes softly, lost in flight.

The leaves respond with whispered sighs,
Beneath the stars that fill the skies.
Each note a tear, a sorrow shared,
In every heart, a story bared.

The moonlit path, a shimmering thread,
Guides the lost where dreams are led.
As silence wraps the world in peace,
A moment's grace, a sad release.

Yet in her song, a glimmer glows,
A light through darkness gently flows.
For every tear that nature weeps,
A new dawn breaks, as night retreats.

So listen close to the nightingale,
Her weeping voice, a tender tale.
In sorrow's depths, hope finds a way,
To weave the night into the day.

Lurking Harmonies of the Underbrush

In shadows deep where secrets hide,
The underbrush, a world inside.
With rustling leaves and whispered calls,
Nature's music softly falls.

A rustle here, a flutter there,
The creatures dance without a care.
Their harmonies, a wild song,
In this haven where they belong.

Among the ferns, a fox takes flight,
While crickets sing into the night.
The symphony of life unfolds,
In every note, a story told.

The moonlight glimmers on the ground,
As whispers in the dark surround.
Each shadow flits, each heartbeat flows,
This hidden world forever grows.

So wander here, where nature plays,
Beneath the sky, through verdant bays.
In lurking harmonies, you'll find,
The pulse of life, intertwined.

Breathing the Sighs of the Unknown

Upon the edge where daylight wanes,
The air is thick with whispered strains.
In every breath, a truth concealed,
The sighs of worlds yet unrevealed.

Each shadow holds a tale untold,
Of wanderers brave and hearts so bold.
They tread the paths where few have dared,
With hopes that flicker, unprepared.

The night embraces secrets deep,
In dreams we sow, in dreams we reap.
The stars above, a distant guide,
As we embark on this strange ride.

With every whisper on the breeze,
We dance beneath the ancient trees.
The sighs of night, they weave and wind,
Through tangled thoughts, our fates aligned.

So breathe it in, this gentle spell,
The sighs of wonder, all is well.
For in the unknown, lies our grace,
A journey bold, we must embrace.

The Charm of Long-Woven Tales

In corners dark where stories bloom,
The charm of tales dispels the gloom.
With every word, a magic spun,
A thread of life, a race begun.

From hearth to heart, these tales will glide,
Through shadowed paths where dreams reside.
In laughter bright or sorrowed sighs,
The wisdom of the ages ties.

With every telling, old and new,
A flicker of hope shines gently through.
The wonders woven in our minds,
A tapestry of humankind.

So gather 'round and lend an ear,
For every tale brings forth a cheer.
In every heart, a story waits,
The charm of long-woven fates.

So let us weave, let voices ring,
In every tale, our spirits sing.
For in their charm, we find our place,
A shared story, a warm embrace.

Echoes of the Shimmering Leaf

In whispers soft, the leaves do dance,
Their tales of old, a fleeting chance.
A glimmer bright in twilight's glow,
With secrets wrapped in silver show.

Through branches thick, the shadows weave,
A tapestry that dreams believe.
The air is thick with magic's song,
Where every heartbeat feels so strong.

Beneath the boughs, the stories sigh,
Of spirits past that linger nigh.
If you but listen, hearts will race,
For nature's laughter finds its place.

Emerald hues in soft moonlight,
A gentle pull, a sweet delight.
In every rustle, soft and clear,
The echoes call, inviting near.

So let us roam this vibrant glade,
Where leaves may whisper, never fade.
With every step, a magic found,
In shimmering peace, our souls unbound.

Ballads of the Waking Fog

When dawn slips in with tender grace,
The fog will rise, a soft embrace.
It blankets all in whispered tales,
Of hidden paths and secret trails.

Through muted light, the world transforms,
As dreams are born in gentle swarms.
Each breath a song, each step a dance,
A chance to lose and find romance.

The sun will chase the mist away,
Yet in its heart, the echoes stay.
For in the fog, our hopes take flight,
In swirling depths, we find our light.

In morning's hush, the magic stirs,
With every whisper, joy occurs.
A ballad sung on whispered breeze,
Transcending time with perfect ease.

So wander forth through muted space,
Where dreams and waking hearts embrace.
In fog's soft arms, we come alive,
In ballads sweet, our spirits thrive.

Celestial Serenades in the Gloom

In twilight's cloak, the stars align,
With whispers soft, their glow divine.
A serenade for hearts that yearn,
In shadowed depths, new dreams will burn.

The moon hangs low, a silver key,
Unlocking nights where spirits flee.
Each note a promise, pure and bright,
In gloomy spaces, dance in light.

The heavens hum a soft refrain,
A melody of joy and pain.
Through cosmic arms, we drift and sway,
In starlit paths, we find our way.

Let us embrace the night's allure,
With every beat, our souls endure.
For within gloom, a magic swells,
In celestial tunes, our spirit tells.

So raise your voice under the skies,
In harmony where silence lies.
In serenades, we lose the gloom,
And celebrate the dreams that bloom.

Dreaming in the Garden of Shadows

In twilight's hush, the shadows play,
In gardens where lost dreams decay.
With every step on ancient ground,
The pulse of secrets can be found.

Through petals soft and creeping vines,
A dance of thoughts, where magic shines.
In every corner, thoughts take flight,
As day surrenders into night.

Beneath the boughs, a hush will grow,
As whispers weave in twilight's glow.
A haven found where echoes cease,
In evening's arms, we find our peace.

Let dreams take root in hidden fears,
In gentle grace, release our tears.
For in the dark, our hopes embrace,
In shadows deep, we find our place.

So linger long, where silence reigns,
In gardens lush, escape the chains.
In dreaming softly, hearts unfold,
In shadows' arms, our stories told.

Tones of Twilight's Embrace

In shadows deep where whispers play,
The stars awaken, dreams hold sway.
A gentle breeze through branches sighs,
As night descends and daylight dies.

The moon casts silver, soft and bright,
Embraced by dark, yet full of light.
Mysteries wrapped in velvet night,
In twilight's glow, the world feels right.

Through calming hues, the colors blend,
A symphony with no clear end.
Each moment held in soft embrace,
With every heartbeat, time leaves trace.

The crickets chirp their nightly song,
Where shadows stretch and night is long.
In quietude, our thoughts take flight,
We wander through the starry night.

So linger here in dusk's sweet grace,
With every twinkle, dreams we chase.
In tones of twilight, spirits rise,
As worlds awaken 'neath dark skies.

Enigma of the Forest's Breath

In forest deep where secrets dwell,
Life whispers soft, a hidden spell.
The leaves conspire with time and air,
In rustling tones, they weave a prayer.

An ancient oak with arms outspread,
Shares tales where light and shadow tread.
Beneath its boughs, the world stands still,
A sacred space that time can't kill.

The murmur of a stream runs clear,
Each droplet sings for those who hear.
The fluttering wings of birds in flight,
Unravel magic, pure delight.

Sunbeams filter through the dense, green veil,
A tapestry of nature's tale.
With every breath, the forest sighs,
In hushed tones where the marvel lies.

So wander on, oh curious heart,
For every path is a work of art.
In the enigma of this sacred place,
Lose yourself in nature's embrace.

Rhythms of the Mystic Canopy

Above the treetops, stars align,
In the canopy, rhythms intertwine.
The world below fades soft and low,
While whispers dance with the moon's glow.

Leaves flutter like the sands of time,
Moments captured in silence, sublime.
Glistening dew, a jewel's grace,
Reflects the dreams we long to trace.

A symphony plays in twilight's charm,
With every note, the soul finds calm.
The wind carries songs of long ago,
Where legends rest and shadows grow.

Beneath the boughs, the magic swells,
In every heartbeat, the forest tells.
The chorus swells with the nightingale,
As moonbeams weave through the misty veil.

So listen close, oh wandering soul,
For in the rhythm, you become whole.
In the mystic canopy's embrace,
Find your dream, find your place.

Ghostly Harmonization of the Ether

In veils of mist where shadows blend,
The echoes dance, the sorrows mend.
A haunting tune, a specter's sigh,
In every note, the past draws nigh.

Through twilight haze, the whispers call,
A timeless song that enchants all.
Ghostly figures in soft moonlight,
Move with the rhythms of the night.

In gentle sways, the memories weave,
A tapestry that none can leave.
The air is thick with tales once spun,
Of love and loss, of battles won.

So linger here where spirits dwell,
In harmonies that weave a spell.
Each breath a note, each heartbeat a chord,
In the ether's song, we find our word.

Embrace the silence, let it flow,
For in the stillness, glimmers grow.
Ghostly whispers, soft and clear,
In the harmonization, we draw near.